THE POWER OF THOUGHT

Core Principles to Overcome
Adversity and Achieve Success

Brandon Webb

"There are people who talk, and people who do."

To my mother and father
for creating a childhood environment that produced a doer.

INTRODUCTION

We learn from stories: some true, some fiction. I've loved stories and storytelling since I was a boy marooned on my family's sailboat, "Agio," for long stretches at sea. I had a bunk room full of books and a large imagination. I was a voracious reader; there were no cell phones back then, and no TV in the middle of the southern Pacific Ocean. I relied on those stories for entertainment, for inspiration. Now, I hope my story entertains and inspires, too.

This is a story of a small boy, scared and alone in the world, who ran away from home at 16, and overcame numerous hostile environments to pursue his dream to become a Navy SEAL, a pilot, a business owner, and a New York Times best-selling author.

People told me I'd never amount to anything as a young man, including my high school counselor in Ojai, California. These people (I call them dream-stealers) invent reasons why we can't or shouldn't pursue our dreams.

This story of mine is true; the experiences are real and raw. There are no chapters; I wrote this book almost nonstop. In keeping with how I wrote it, it's one continuous story, presented the same way it spilled out of me and onto my MacBook Air as I sat surrounded by the dark ocean night outside my San Juan condominium.

There are plenty of recent studies that prove the benefits of positive psychology. This isn't one of them. While I truly believe in the benefits of positive psychology, and focusing on desired outcomes, I also know that people learn by sharing experiences, good and bad. Sharing experiences rather than prescriptive advice is like giving someone the tools they need to problem solve on their own and become successful. It reminds me of the quotation, "Give a man a fish and you feed him for a day; teach a man to fish, and you feed him for a lifetime."

In my experience, sharing personal stories can be the wind that blows away the fog surrounding an otherwise clear and ever-present solution. My hope is that, in reading *The Power of Thought*, you'll learn the importance of taking time to think and speak to yourself more powerfully.

THE POWER OF THOUGHT

I was born east of Vancouver in the Canadian Rockies to an American mom and a Canadian dad. (Don't worry, I don't plan on running for president!) My parents were hippies, met in California, and my dad moved my mom to Canada (he's originally from the Toronto area). There, they had me and my sister. I'll spare you the crazy details and just give you the abridged version. If you want the full story, read my memoir, *The Red Circle*.

I was a terror as a young kid. So bad, in fact, my mom actually called social services on herself because I was driving her *that* crazy. Yes, she reported herself. It was bad.

My dad is a great craftsman, and carved (literally and metaphorically) out a construction company amidst the hard Rocky Mountain landscape. He became very successful, then lost it all. It was tough on the whole family and ended in total bankruptcy. I would experience something similar later in life. The apple doesn't fall far from the tree.

My parents then decided to buy a sailboat and save up to take us all on some crazy sailing adventures. We bought a '47 Ketch, sailed it from Seattle down to Ventura, California, where we lived on the boat for a few years. Being a boat kid in California must be like growing up in a trailer park in Texas. You get made fun of, but hey, it builds character, right?

We took a quick trip to Mexico on our boat when I was 11, and it was an incredible adventure. Then, back to school and Ventura.

My mom put me into sports to keep me out of trouble, but eventually I developed Osgood–Schlatter disease (It's not as bad as it sounds!) and had to give up sports. That's when I got a job working on a SCUBA-diving boat called the *Peace*, based out of Ventura Harbor. It was a great job for a 12-year-old kid. I ended up spending most of my early teens on the boat becoming a competent diver and deckhand. Eventually, I began earning good money, really good money for a 15-year-old kid. Then my dad hit me with it: We were going to sail to Australia.

"Shoot!" I thought, "I don't want to do that!" I was young, making great money, and I just wanted to chase girls and get my driver's license. But off I went, the reluctant crew member.

We made it as far as Tahiti before my dad and I were at each other's throats. I was an experienced boatsman with a chip on my shoulder, and it was in Tahiti where I learned really quickly that there was only one captain, and it was not me. My dad and I agreed that I, having finished my junior year of high school early, would get off the boat for good.

So, as we say in the Navy, "No sh*t, there I was...." Alone and afraid at 16 years old.

I found a boat that needed help crewing back to Hawaii. I cried myself to sleep the first couple nights away from my floating home and my family. It was tough, but sometimes tough love is needed.

Once we reached Hilo, Hawaii, I flew back to California. It was there that I finished high school while working part time on a dive boat and at my friend's dive shop. Then, watching my friends from the dive boat get into trouble and drugs, I knew I needed to get out of that environment. We are who we hang out with, and I needed to make a change. So I joined the Navy. There's much more to the story, but that's the short version.

I joined the Navy to be a SEAL, and just about everyone I knew at the time thought I was crazy. Still, my mom and dad believed in me, especially my father, and that meant a lot.

Take note, parents: Always believe in your kids. It matters. How you talk to them, what you say about them when you think you're out of earshot, matters. It influences how they think about themselves and and what they think is possible. Remember that.

So I joined the Navy, and signed up for the aircrew search and rescue program because I didn't know any better, and because at the time they had no direct route to SEAL training (they do now, thank goodness).

The following is an excerpt from my first book, *The Red Circle,* and gives you an idea of what it took for me to just get a shot at attending SEAL training. It takes place after I finished Navy boot camp (Orlando, Florida), aircrew school, search-and-rescue school (Pensacola, Florida), and aviation warfare systems operator training ("AW" training in Memphis, Tennessee). After these schools, I was selected for a West Coast helicopter squadron at Naval Air Station North Island in San Diego, California.

For those of you who've read the book before, stop the eye-rolling; this isn't some trick to get you to read a bunch of my first book again. I just want to get everyone caught up to the point in my Navy career where I really started to learn the value of powerful thinking. So if you've read my first book, just think of this as a friendly conversation to get you reacquainted with the story.

So here I was in San Diego, California, as a fresh-faced 19-year-old kid with the world ahead of him. I had just finished eating bugs and getting my ass kicked in a mock prisoner-of-war camp during SERE School (survive, evade, escape, resist). I was no longer Petty Officer Webb, I was "War Criminal 53!" What a great time and experience. It still brings a smile to my face all these years later.

———————◆———————

At the end of January, I got about a week to recover from survival school, then classed up in an advanced program called "C" school, where I spent the next three months learning the advanced sonar concepts that were the theoretical foundation of the "antisubmarine warfare" sonar operator's trade.

During these three months I began to get a taste of just how much complex knowledge and technical know-how I would be absorbing over my years in the military. For weeks at a stretch, we pored over material in courses with names like Electronic Warfare, Oceanography, Advanced Acoustic Analysis, and Aural Listening. Just two years earlier I'd been a teenager struggling my way through high school math. Now I was absorbing all kinds of advanced concepts and academic material and, oddly enough, doing so without breaking a sweat. The simple truth was, it was fascinating. It had to do with tracking things underwater—something I had no trouble relating to.

In "A" school we had learned the basics of reading submarine acoustic signatures. Now we really dove into the subject, pouring hours into studying the harmonic frequencies emitted by bodies in the water.

As you descend farther down, the water changes temperature; however, it does not do so gradually, along a smooth continuum, but in discrete chunks, something like a layer cake. I knew this from experience, because you can feel these temperature breaks as you dive. As I now learned, these distinct temperature layers are called thermoclines. The interesting thing about these layers is that they trap sound, and consequently the way sound waves travel is dictated to some degree by the layout of thermoclines: As a sound wave hits the bottom of a thermocline (or, depending on how you're looking at it, the top of the one below it), it then spreads outward, trapped within that layer of depth.

Because of this, if you have a submarine hiding down at, say, 50 feet, you're not necessarily going to hear it if you (or your sonar buoy) are at 30 feet. In other words, submarines can literally hide within thermoclines. If the vessel makes enough noise, it may create sufficient energy to bleed through into the next layer—but a modern submarine is so stealthy that you have to be in that thermocline to hear it. I filed this information away; a few years later I would use it to my advantage in a most unexpected circumstance.

I made it through "C" school uneventfully—with one exception.

Since I would be spending at least the next few years of my life here in San Diego, I wanted to make sure I could keep up with two of my favorite pastimes, surfing and spearfishing. While in "C" school, we had ample time off for extracurricular activities, so I went up to my mom's place in Ventura, got a surfboard and one of my spear guns out of storage, and brought them back down with me to Coronado.

One day, coming back from class to my barracks room, I found a note saying that my room had been inspected and I needed to come to the military police HQ to pick up my spear gun. Thinking nothing of it, I grabbed a jacket and headed off.

When I arrived at HQ, I was promptly arrested. The charge: possession of a deadly weapon on base. They put me in a holding cell.

I could not believe what was happening. Possession of a deadly weapon—were they kidding me? I was a diver, for Heaven's sake. Spearfishing was what I did. And I obviously wasn't trying to hide the spear gun. I couldn't have even I'd wanted to: It was too big to fit in my locker. I'd had it lying out in the open. Were they serious?

They were. The MPs acted like jackasses, doing their best to intimidate me and impress upon me that I had screwed up big time, that my Navy career was over.

Yeah, yeah. Bite me.

They called one of the chiefs who happened to be on duty at my school and told him what was going on. To my great relief, as soon as he showed up they remanded me into his custody. My relief soon turned to surprise: The moment the chief and I were alone together, he started laying into me. I knew enough to keep my mouth shut and just take his shit, but it seemed strange and a little silly that they were making such a big deal out of it.

The rest of the instructor staff at "C" school thought the whole thing was pretty funny, and they gave me quite a lot of crap about it, as did all my classmates. When it came time to graduate, they all got together and created a special "Jacques Cousteau" award for the poor slob who got arrested for possession of a spear gun. I still have that award. I never got my spear gun back.

The day after graduation, one of the other chiefs called me into his office. He told me he didn't agree with the way the first chief had handled the situation. "You're a diver and a spear-fisherman, Webb," he said. "I respect that, and I'm sorry the Navy confiscated your spear gun."

"Yes, Chief," was all I said, but it felt good to have someone in a leadership position say what he did. I could understand their need to enforce the rules. But I was still angry about it. They had destroyed a perfectly good spear gun.

It wasn't the last time I'd see what seemed to me examples of good leadership and poor leadership side by side. It also wasn't the last time I'd find myself in trouble.

In April, fresh out of "C" school, I was assigned to HS-10, the helicopter training squadron where I would spend the next six months learning how to function as an aircrew member and operate the systems in the back of assorted types of H-60 helicopter.

The H-60 is a broad class of U.S. military helicopters that includes the Seahawk, the Oceanhawk, the famous Blackhawk, and a handful of others. At HS-10 they put us into several different kinds of simulators representing the various helicopter platforms we would soon be flying. One had a heavy sonar package; another, which we called a truck, was completely gutted out and used mainly for combat and search-and-rescue exercises.

After learning all the technology on the simulators, it was time to go out on live trainings. They put one instructor in front with the pilot and another instructor in back with the air crewmen. Here they taught us how to operate the hoist, how to use the proper terminology to talk from the front to the back, radio etiquette, all the different systems on the aircraft.

In mid-October, after six months at the helo training squadron, I got orders to the Helicopter Anti-Submarine Squadron Six. HS-6, also known as the Indians, was my first actual deployment. Yes, I was still in training—but I was now part of an actual, operational helicopter command. I was in the Navy fleet now.

And a helluva command it was. The squadron had an illustrious history stretching back nearly 40 years. The Indians had rescued more than a dozen downed pilots in Vietnam and helped UDT teams (the predecessors of SEALs) pluck moon-walking Apollo astronauts out of the ocean on splashdown, had earned a long succession of trophies and awards, and would years later go on to serve the efforts in Afghanistan and Iraq. I was excited about becoming part of HS-6. It was a damn good squadron, and I was out to make a name for myself.

Back in April, when I had first arrived at HS-10 for training, I had made another strong push to get orders to SEAL training. Once again, I'd been told I would have to wait until I got to my final duty station. Well, here I was, at my final duty station, and I was determined to do a kick-ass job so I could apply for BUD/S (Basic, Underwater, Demolition, SEAL) and get the hell out of there as fast as I could.

Which turned out not to be very fast at all. In fact, I would continue serving as part of the Indians from October 1994 through the summer of 1997, encountering obstacle after obstacle in my quest, before finally getting my orders to SEAL training nearly three full years later. In the spring of 1995, about six months after becoming part of the Indians, I went on a six-month deployment on the aircraft carrier USS Abraham Lincoln in the western Pacific, called a WESTPAC. An aircraft carrier normally sports a full-time crew of several thousand. When it leaves port for a WESTPAC, though, all its associated helicopter squadrons populate it and disembark with it, which brings the total on-board population up to around 5,000, and it becomes like a small city unto itself.

We had gone out before for shorter trips of up to a month. The WESTPAC was different. Now we headed out west, clear across the Pacific, stopping in Hawaii, Hong Kong, Thailand, Australia, and then on to the Persian Gulf, where we spent the next four or five months as the U.S. aircraft carrier presence there. This was something like being a cop on the beat. We weren't necessarily engaging anyone or seeing any action, but we were the show of force, ready to be tapped for whatever need might arise.

For those of us still in training, the WESTPAC gave us the opportunity to learn everything we could ever want to know about all the systems on the different helo platforms we were using at the time. But for me, it meant one thing: earning as many qualifications as possible so I could get to BUD/S. As great as life was in the squadron, I wanted nothing more than to get the hell out of there, the sooner the better.

At the center of BUD/S training there is a monstrosity I'd heard about called the O-course, a brutally difficult setup aimed at developing superhuman endurance while inflicting maximum punishment. Later on, when I finally got the chance to face the actual O-course, it would nearly beat me. Meanwhile, I decided that if I kept facing obstacles in my path, I would treat them as my own private O-course and use them to make me stronger.

The problem with letting people know I wanted to go into SEAL training was that everyone knew about the absurd attrition rate at BUD/S, where typically some 80 percent wash out. To make matters worse, the aircrew community has a terrible reputation for sending in guys who wash out more than 90 percent of the time. This made my life pretty rough at HS-6. By this time, though, I'd figured out that when people tell you that you can't do something, you can use it to your advantage, and every time someone else told me I was crazy and would never make it to BUD/S (let alone through BUD/S), I was determined to use it as more motivational fuel. My operational philosophy was, "I'm just going to do the best job I can and get all the quals, and then they'll let me go."

And right now, that meant getting my Tactical Sensor Operator (TSO) qual.

Over the course of our deployment on the USS Lincoln, I completed all the requirements I needed in order to take my TSO test. The TSO ran the show and was the senior guy in the back of the aircraft. In essence, this would mean getting my qualification for crew chief. One September day, toward the end of that WESTPAC, the time finally came for my first check ride. Pass this, and I would have that crew chief qual I needed. I was ready to go and totally psyched.

"Check ride" means exactly that: From the moment we lifted off the flight deck and flew out over the Gulf, they checked every move I made, testing me on everything—language and terminology, correct procedures and sequences, how I operated every system I touched. If you're tracking a submarine, for example, then you're managing the sonar and making decisions in the back. If you're on a rescue operation to pull a downed pilot out of the drink, then the level of control intensifies. As sonar operator, once you're in search-and-rescue mode on the scene of a recovery operation, the pilot toggles hover control over to you and you are running the show. In a sense, I had to demonstrate that I could function as a pilot, too.

The entire check ride lasted about two hours. We touched down on the flight deck, and I turned to my instructors to get their feedback.

"You did pretty well," they said. "But you need more experience."

I stared at them, stunned. They were flunking me.

Technically speaking, I actually had passed the minimum requirements of the check ride, and I knew it as well as they did. But the instructors are given some latitude in the scoring process, and there were a few senior guys in the squadron who were not exactly looking out for me. In the course of our deployment, I had knocked out all the requirements so fast that it kind of freaked a few of them out, and they wanted to see me cut down to size.

I didn't argue, but I was annoyed as hell. Now I had a negative mark on my record. In retrospect I realize that I shoulder some of the blame here: I had probably pushed too hard to take the test before being fully ready for it. But if they'd already decided I wasn't ready, then why did they let me take the test?

A few days later an event occurred that gave me one of the most vivid experiences in my life of great leadership and terrible leadership, side by side.

We were out on nighttime maneuvers over the Persian Gulf. Our pilot that night, Lieutenant Bennett, was the sort of officer you can't help disliking: a slimy guy who alienated officers and enlisted men alike. Lt. Bennett's copilot, Kennedy, was a good guy and quite smart, though a little on the geeky side. Rich Fries and I both served as crewmen; Rich was senior to me. In terms of rank and experience, I was the low man on this totem pole.

It had been a long night, and in order to make it all the way back to the Lincoln, we had to stop and refuel on a nearby destroyer. The night was pretty calm but visibility was against us, as there was absolutely no moon out, and it was damn close to pitch black out there.

A destroyer's deck is pretty tight to land on, especially as compared to an aircraft carrier like the USS Lincoln, and even more so at night with such low visibility. Because of this, it was common operating procedure to slow the helo down to 90 knots (just over 100 mph), then open the cabin door and have one of the crewman spot the deck, that is, assist the pilot with verbal commands. On this occasion, the crewman doing the spotting was me.

As the helo slowed down to under 90 knots, I passed a message over the ICS (internal communication system) that the door was coming open. The door cracked open and I looked out to get a visual on the destroyer's lights. For some reason, I couldn't make anything out. I kept straining to see something, and finally caught a glimpse of light—but it was at eye level, which I thought was strange. I looked down and realized that we were not where we were supposed to be. We were not slowly descending and approaching the deck. Our pilot had put us down at water level.

We were about to crash into the ocean.

"Altitude! Altitude!" I yelled. All hell broke loose. Rich immediately realized what was happening and joined in with me. And I will never, in all my life, forget what happened next. Suddenly we heard Lt. Bennett's voice shrilly piercing through our yells: "What's happening?!" he screamed. "I don't know what's happening! Oh God, oh God!"

And he kept repeating that. Oh God, oh God.

For a split second Rich and I gaped at each other in disbelief. This was our pilot. This was our aircraft commander. And he was screaming like a frightened schoolgirl.

We were done for. I held tight onto the cabin door. By now there was a foot of seawater in the main cabin, and any second we would be swamped and overrun with ocean: the point of no return. In my mind's eye, I could see the rotor blades sabering into the water and splintering into a thousand pieces, the helo flipping upside down and sinking into the Gulf. Everything slowed way down and a stream of contrasting thoughts tore through my mind:

"This is why we go through the helo dunker training blindfolded."

"Is this is really how it's going to end?"

"No—I am not going to let this jackass Bennett kill me!"

And then something happened that turned it all around in an instant. Kennedy, our copilot, somehow torqued his shit together and hauled us and that damned helo up and out of the water. It was inches short of miraculous. Hell, maybe it was miraculous.

The crew on the destroyer thought we had crashed and that for sure we were goners, when suddenly they were shocked and thrilled to see us popping back up on radar.

Rich immediately replaced me on the door, exactly as he should have (he was senior to me and had thousands of hours in the H60 under his belt), and he rapidly talked Kennedy down onto the deck after a few missed approaches. Bennett was an utter disaster the entire time, mumbling to himself like a street person with a drug habit.

Despite our reports, nobody on the destroyer believed that we had actually put the bird into the drink. Not, that is, until the maintenance chief tore the tail section apart—and seawater started pouring out. A short investigation followed but it went nowhere. The CO of HS-6 didn't want his career to end over this incident, and he kept things tightly under wraps.

I don't know how he did it, but Kennedy saved all our lives that night, and he deserved a medal for it. But that wasn't what happened. Instead, both Bennett and Kennedy had their Helicopter Aircraft Commander (HAC) papers suspended. Kennedy, the guy who had saved us all with his heroism and remarkable calm under pressure, got punished right along with Bennett, the guy who cracked apart like an eggshell and nearly guaranteed our watery demise.

I came away from that near-disaster with a resolve never to judge a person based on appearance. Kennedy had always seemed like a smart and very competent guy, but not one I would have figured for a hero. You never know what a person is capable of until you get to work with them, side by side.

I hope I get the chance to shake his hand again one day.

In the long run, my fast-track-to-BUD/S strategy backfired on me. I had thought that if I gave everything my best, I would prove to my superiors that I was a hard worker and they would approve my package to BUD/S. In fact, the opposite happened. The better I did, the more valuable I was to my superiors—and the more reluctant they were to let me go.

And when I say they, who I'm really talking about is Chief Brian Carnely.

Chief Carnely was an East-Coast guy who hated being out on the West Coast and among what he described as "the fruit loops." When he looked at me and some of my buddies, all he saw was guys who spent their whole lives surfing: We were all slackers. A few guys in the shop sucked up to him. Nobody else could stand him. To this day, I am amazed that this guy made chief and was put in charge of an aircrew shop. Carnely was a walking, talking, textbook illustration of how not to lead. He played favorites and rewarded people he liked, based not on any accomplishments but purely on the fact that he happened to like them. And the guys he happened to like the most were also those who did the least amount of work and continually dragged down the rest of us.

In March 1996, about five months after returning from the USS Lincoln WESTPAC, I submitted my first BUD/S package, that is, my application along with all the necessary supporting documentation. It was quickly denied.

Instinctively, I knew that Carnely had screwed me. It was only months later that I would learn in full detail what had actually happened.

In order for me to get out of my AW job and get orders to BUD/S, permission needed to come from the appropriate rating detailer, the person who controls where people transfer to or work next to in the Navy. As it happened, our rating detailer was a man with the mind-blowingly unfortunate name of Petty Officer A. W. Dickover. (Someone, somewhere, must have seen the humor in this and assigned him the job based on his name alone.) Chief Carnely had put in a call to Petty Officer Dickover and asked him not to approve my request for orders to SEAL training.

You are probably wondering how I learned what had happened. I learned it because Carnely himself actually admitted to me what he'd done.

The truth was, I was the only third class petty officer in the squadron who was NATOPS-qualified (Naval Air Training and Operating Procedures Standardization), which meant I could do things like giving annual qualification tests. By this point, when it came time for people's annual quals or if someone wanted to test to become a crew chief, I was the one giving them the test. After failing that first check ride, it hadn't taken me long to test again—and pass. But now my rapid advancement came back to bite me.

"You have all these quals," Carnely said. "Sorry, Webb, but I need you for this deployment."

The son of a bitch. Now I would have to stay with the squadron for at least another year and do a whole other six-month WESTPAC deployment.

A few months later, in July, I applied to attend a one-week pre-SEAL selection course, held at the Navy's boot camp facility in Michigan, called Naval Station Great Lakes (or as it's unofficially called, Great Mistakes). This is not a pass/fail kind of course and going through it wouldn't give me any technical qualification. Still, depending on how I did, I could come out of it with a recommendation to the real BUD/S—or without one. In a sense, it would be an informal entrance exam. If I flew through pre-BUD/S, it would boost my chances of getting orders to the real deal. And if I couldn't make it through the week at Great Mistakes, I could forget about surviving the seven months of the genuine article.

Calling pre-BUD/S a condensed version of the real thing would be a stretch. It is designed to give you a glimpse of what the actual BUD/S training experience would be like, but only a glimpse. I knew that. Still, it was one way to demonstrate that I was serious, and hopefully I would come out of it with an endorsement.

There was a mix of guys in the program, some straight out of boot camp, some who were already regular Navy, like me. One guy there cut an especially intimidating figure: a six-foot-tall, blond, Nordic-looking dude whom I'll call "Lars." Lars had thighs like *tree trunks and could do pushups from sunup to sunrise. He just crushed everything they threw at him. I met up with Lars again a year later when I finally made it to BUD/S, and will have more to say about him at that point.*

I passed the program with flying colors, and they recommended me for BUD/S. But my obstacle course wasn't over yet.

After he admitted to his duplicity in tanking my first BUD/S package, Chief Carnely and I had for the most part stayed out of each other's way. Our mutual animosity came to a head, though, during my second WESTPAC deployment, which started in October of 1996. I had now been part of HS-6 for exactly two years, and I was determined to make it to BUD/S before another full year went by. I submitted a second BUD/S package and was pretty confident that it would go through. After all, I had done the pre-BUD/S course and had come out with a strong recommendation.

However, I also knew that if I wanted to pass the entrance qualifications for BUD/S when I got back stateside, I needed to get into shape. On the aircraft carrier, it was hard to keep up high fitness standards: I couldn't swim, I couldn't really run (running on a steel deck is not exactly great for the joints), and getting in a full workout routine was difficult. Six months in those conditions would really set me back.

I went to Chief Carnely and told him my situation.

"Don't worry," he said, "I'll send you back on early detachment (that is, guys who were flown back early to prepare the home command for the rest of the group's return). In fact, I'll send you back a month early, so you can train and get in shape before you have to qualify."

I was a little surprised and quite grateful that he would go out of his way to do this. But he was lying through his teeth. He never had any intention of sending me back home early. He didn't want me to go to BUD/S and was determined to prevent it from happening, whatever that took.

A few weeks later, a friend in our squadron admin took me aside and told me I was getting railroaded (Navyspeak for screwed over) by Chief Carnely on my upcoming evaluation.

Evaluations go a long way in making rank in the Navy: In addition to taking a rating test, your evals are added into the mix, yielding a final multiple that determines whether or not you are promoted. Normally you would not have a chance to see how your peers break out during an evaluation period unless you exchange notes. Through my friend, I learned that I was being rated as low as the brand new check-ins.

I was not about to take that lying down. If I had deserved a low eval, that would be one thing—but that was clearly not the case. I had busted my ass to get every qual I possibly could and volunteered for every shit detail to prove to my peers and superiors that I deserved a shot at BUD/S.

Here's how the process works: After receiving your written eval and having a one-on-one debrief with whoever wrote it, you sign your name at the bottom. There is a tiny box there by the signature line that you check if you intend to submit a statement along with your eval. Hardly anyone ever marks a check in that box. I still remember the look of utter horror on Chief Carnely's face when he saw me check the box. He knew that I knew what he was up to. He knew he had fucked up.

At the time I was taking a few college classes on the ship (they even had professors on board: As I said, an aircraft carrier is like a small city) and had just finished English 1302. I thought this would be a prime opportunity to put my writing skills to use. I prepared a formal statement, which I took great care in writing. It contained not a single whine or complaint, nothing but the facts, line item by line item.

Apparently, my statement created quite a stir. After it landed on my department head's desk, he ran it up to the commanding officer. Pretty soon I got word that Chief Carnely and I were both wanted in Commander Rosa's office.

When I arrived, Carnely was already there. I nodded at him without a word. It was obvious that he was not too happy with the situation. Chiefs run the Navy, and in the Navy culture, it is extremely rare for anyone to go against a chief or question his judgment or leadership. But I would be damned if I was going to roll over and take this. Maybe this came from my time on the dive boat, when I often felt I had to prove myself to guys who were all older than me. Maybe it was an echo of the times I stood up to my dad— or maybe I got it from my dad, and it reflects the times he stood up to his father. Whatever its source, there is a stubborn streak in me that refuses to knuckle under to what seems to me a poor decision or unfair judgment.

We were both ushered into Commander Rosa's office, where we stood for a moment while the commander continued looking down at his desk at the eval and written statement spread out in front of him. He looked up at me, then at Chief Carnely, then back at me. "Look," he said to me, "what's the deal here?"

"Sir," I said, "in block 1, Professional Knowledge, I should be rated a 3.0. I'm the only guy in my shop who has these quals."

The rating system went from 1.0, "Below standards," to 4.0, "Greatly exceeds standards." I had been qualified as a NATOPS instructor, and at the time I was the only third class petty officer in the squad who had done so. It's hard enough for a senior guy to get this qual, let alone a junior guy. And I wasn't even asking for a 4.0, just a 3.0, "Above standards." Carnely had rated me with a 2.0: "Progressing."

Commander Rosa looked at each of us again in turn, saying nothing, his face reddening. The chief looked like an idiot. It was clear that he had given me this poor rating purely because he didn't like me.

The CO turned back to me and said, "Petty Officer Webb, if the chief can't figure this out, you write your own eval." He paused, then said, "That's all."

We were both free to go.

I did not leave the WESTPAC early, but was kept on for the full six months. Not long after this encounter, Chief Carnely transferred out of HS-6. We did not stay in touch.

My experience on those two WESTPAC tours taught me another powerful lesson about leadership, great and lousy.

When I had first deployed on the USS Lincoln, back in May of 1995, it didn't take long to realize that morale on the ship was generally horrible. "This ship stinks," I heard people say. And it was true. It was unkempt and funky. Everyone hated being there.

The strangest thing happened on the Lincoln: For a few weeks, there was a pervert running around. This guy, whoever he was, would come quietly up to the door of a female crew's room, slip one hand inside the door, hit the lights—then run in, cop a quick *feel, and run out again. It freaked us all out. This was the kind of thing you might expect on a college campus, and even there it would be creepy. But on a Navy fighting vessel?!*

And here is the most bizarre thing about it: They never caught him. Nobody ever knew who it was. In a way, it was ridiculous, almost absurd. But it was also unnerving, not only for the women, who never knew when the guy would show up, but for the rest of us, too. And in a weird way, the episode underlined that pervasive queasy sense that the place was never under tight command.

The following year, when my second WestPac deployment came around, I dreaded it. This time we would be stationed on the USS Kitty Hawk. This old boat was not a spanking new nuclear vessel like the Lincoln; it was a conventionally powered ship that had been around since Vietnam. When our squadron deployed onto its deck, my heart sank. Hey, I figured, if the brand new ship was such a shitty experience, then this one was going to be downright awful.

But it wasn't. In fact, it was the opposite. The moment I was onboard the Kitty Hawk I could feel the difference. It was clean. The crew was happy. Everything hummed along. This place was wired tight.

It didn't take long to understand why. That first night I was surprised to hear the captain of the Kitty Hawk come over the PA loudspeaker, welcoming us and giving us a brief rundown of what was happening that day.

This never happened on the Lincoln. The captain of that vessel hardly ever talked to his crew. Never said a goddamn word. It was weeks, months before we ever heard his voice over that PA system, and that happened maybe twice during the entire six-month stretch.

But not on the Kitty Hawk. It wasn't just the first day that the captain addressed us. He did it again the next day, and the next, and every one of the roughly 180 days we were aboard his ship.

"Good afternoon shipmates, this is your captain," the familiar voice would say, "this is what we're doing, here's where we're going, these are the decisions we're making...." He never revealed any details or specific plans that he shouldn't have, but he made sure that everyone felt included in what we were doing.

The difference this made was amazing. It may have been a much older vessel, but it was spotless. Morale was consistently high.

The two experiences were like night and day, and the difference came down to a single factor: Captain Steven John Tomaszesk and the leadership he brought to the ship's crew. That crew loved their captain because he took care of them, and they knew it. I would have ridden that boat to the gates of Hell with Captain Tomaszesk, and I'm pretty sure every single person on that boat felt the same way.

This was a lesson I would see played out again and again, and it's one I have striven to embody every day, whether it was running a covert op in Afghanistan or Iraq, reorganizing the SEAL sniper course in the States, or in business since getting out of the service. People need to be talked to and kept in the loop.

Years later, I often found myself reflecting back on the lesson of the two captains. The importance of talking to your people, sharing the plan with them so they know where you're headed, and the purpose behind it. It's not rocket science. Engage your crew. Have a dialogue, let them know you know they exist and that they're part of what you're all up to. Leaving people in a vacuum is no way to lead, yet it's a mistake I've seen made way too many times.

When I got back from that second WESTPAC in April of '97, there were orders waiting for me at North Island. I was elated. It had been more than four years since first setting foot in Orlando for boot camp, and after a seemingly endless stream of obstacles, I was finally on my way to BUD/S.

I joined the Navy to be a SEAL. Command after command, I asked to apply, each time getting the same answer. No. Then, when I was eligible, I still got denied! But I kept at it, thinking (yes, thinking) to myself that I was meant to be a SEAL, visualizing myself succeeding. Finally, after all the people who told me I'd never get a shot, here I was, orders in hand.

The following is an excerpt from *The Red Circle* about one of my toughest and most memorable moments of training. To catch you up to this spot, I had checked in horribly out of shape by SEAL standards, and was one of the main guys in a class of 220 students who stood out like a hobo at a country club. My first five weeks of training had been utter horror up to this point: My bones ached to the core, my hands had become calloused from climbing ropes and doing hundreds of pull-ups, and the callouses had then all ripped off, leaving nickel-sized areas of exposed flesh that healed up with sand still trapped inside. My back also ached, and my ribs were sore. The climax of my inglorious five weeks of performance came when I fell off the big obstacle called "The Slide for Life" on the main obstacle course.

It's a three-story climb up, then at the top, you mount the rope, hanging only by your arms with heels crossed over, and begin to inchworm your way down. My grip strength was nonexistent at that point, I stopped to rest, hooked my elbows over the big rope, got yelled at to stop doing that, continued to inch down, and then fell off the rope. First my grip gave, then I hung upside down for a few seconds. I was staring at sand, and an instructor who was angrily eyeing me with a glint in his eye, surely from the anticipation of what he knew was about to come next: me falling three stories. I didn't disappoint. I hit with a thud. Luckily, I had no broken bones (happens to a lot of guys). He asked if I was OK, and I responded with a weak "Hooyah" (BUD/S speak for yes, and a lot of other things). He said, "Good, then get up and move out!"

So here I was, a while later, at another low point. I was about to learn another important lesson about perseverance, and the importance of how we think of and talk to ourselves. Enjoy this final excerpt from *The Red Circle*.

———— ◆ ————

By about the fifth week of Phase One, I was a wreck: exhausted, humiliated, just about beaten into a corner. Then one afternoon, just a few days before Hell Week was to begin, it all came to a head.

Every afternoon we formed up in seven-man boat crews, grabbed our heavy rubber boats, threw them up on top of our heads, and ran with them to the beach to get tortured for a while. On this particular afternoon, we were on our way out to the beach when Instructor Shoulin called over to my team. "Webb, get over here."

Matthews, my boat crew leader, said, "Hey, what's up, Instructor Shoulin? Where is he going?"

"Don't worry about Webb," he replied. "Just go get your fucking boat ready." I looked over and realized that Getka, Buchanan, and Gillespie were all with him. Uh-oh. I peeled away from my boat crew and headed with them out to a section of beach where it was just us, alone: me and the four alpha instructors.

"Drop, Webb," said one of them. "Eight-counts, begin." This was one of their favorite forms of punishment. The eight-count bodybuilder goes like this:

1. Start from a standing position.
2. Drop to a squat, hands on ground.
3. Push legs back to basic push-up position.
4. Execute a push-up.
5. Scissor-kick your legs apart.
6. Legs back together in push-up position.
7. Pull your legs up to your chest.
8. Jump back up to standing position.

They had me do a hundred of these babies, then took me through push-ups, flutter-kicks, the whole works, and all the while they were shoveling sand in my face and yelling at me, all four of them, at the tops of their lungs.

"You are a worthless piece of shit, Webb! Do you even know what a piece of shit you are? You are the biggest piece of shit we've ever seen! You're weighing your whole class down. You are a one-man walking disaster. You are fucking it up for everyone else. You don't belong here, you fleet piece of shit. Do you even know how badly you're fucking this up, how much every one wants you gone? You're a disgrace, Webb. You're garbage. You need to quit. Nobody wants you in Hell Week."

And on and on for the next hour. It was beyond brutal. I could feel how intensely they all wanted me to get up, limp away, and go ring that goddam brass bell.

The worst of it was, I knew they were right. There was a reason they were singling me out. I was physically out of shape and that had been affecting the entire class. And that bothered me. In fact, this is something I've continued to be conscious of and careful about to this day: If you show up late, if you don't have your gear together, or your facts together, or whatever shit it is you need to have together, then you are affecting the whole team. They were right, and it was a lesson I would never forget.

But if I was not physically as tough as I needed to be, I had one thing going for me. I was very tough mentally.

There is a common misperception that to make it through SEAL training you have to be a super athlete. Not so. In its purely physical requirements, the course is designed for the average athletic male to be able to make it through. What SEAL training really tests is your mental mettle. It is designed to push you mentally to the brink, over and over again, until you are hardened and able to take on any task with confidence, regardless of the odds—or until you break.

And I was not about to break.

My body at this point was nowhere near as conditioned as it would become in the months and years ahead. But mentally, I was ready for anything. That was the only reason I survived that hour on the beach. That was the only reason I made it through BUD/S. The power of thought.

People have asked if I ever thought about quitting during the SEAL training, if I ever had one of those dark-night-of-the-soul moments you hear about, those moments of piercing doubt and anguished uncertainty. The answer is, never—not once. But lying there face-down in the sand with these four hard-case psychopaths doing their level best to break me, something else happened instead: I got what we call a fire in the gut.

Of the four, it was Instructor Buchanan who was the most in my face. So I looked up at him, nailed him with the coldest stare I could muster, and said, "Screw you, Instructor Buchanan—screw you. The only way you're getting me out of here is in a body bag."

He glared back at me, gauging me, weighing my intent. I meant every word, and he knew it. He took one step back and jerked his head, gesturing up the beach toward where my boat crew was prepped and waiting. "Get back to your crew," was what he said, but the way he said it made it sound like, "The hell with you."

From that point on, even throughout Hell Week, my experience in BUD/S completely turned the corner. Those instructors left me alone. When Hell Week started a few days later, it felt almost anticlimactic. "Welcome to my world," is what I felt like saying to the other guys. I'd been playing these games throughout First Phase.

There is a saying in BUD/S: Ideally, you want to become the gray man. In other words, you become invisible, nobody notices you, because you do everything so perfectly that you never stand out.

From that point forward, I went from being that *guy to being* the *gray man.*

This was a pivotal point in my life, one that would plant a very small seed that would later begin to grow strong roots, and ultimately become my own personal oak tree of self-thought. The mind is so powerful, I truly believe every human being has it in them to use the power of thought to heal, be strong, overcome adversity, love, be happy, and accomplish our goals in life.

Fast forward a bit. I made it through SEAL training, though it was incredibly tough. Other than being a parent, it was one of the most difficult experiences of my life—and also one of the most rewarding.

I remember going back to HS-6 to visit friends, and hearing all the former naysayers pat me on the back and say, "I knew you would make it all along!" Sure you did, I thought to myself.

Well, what can you do? Sometimes you just have to let it go and accept stuff humbly. I was not there to spike the football.

I finished SEAL training, then went to the Army's basic parachute course in Georgia, and then checked into my first SEAL team.

My first command was SEAL Team 3; it was a great team with a great culture, responsible for southwest Asia—mainly the Middle East. Out of all the teams (with the exception of Team 4, which was responsible for South America), we were actually getting to work at a time when not much was happening elsewhere in the world.

I'm proud to have served at Team 3. It's also where I met my best friend, Glen Doherty, who was one of the heroes of Benghazi who died protecting his fellow Americans while working for the CIA. It was also where I met "American Sniper" Chris Kyle. That command produced some great SEALs.

I served in two SEAL platoons during my career, and my second platoon was deployed to Afghanistan a short time after 9/11. We were one of the first SEAL platoons to operate there. It was an incredible experience to actually put my training to the test in a real combat environment. But war is a terrible thing, one of the worst things we can do to each other as human beings. It's unimaginable. It's unfortunate that we still live in a world that requires good to fight so much evil, but that's still the case and it cannot be ignored.

I was proud of the work we did over there, but my most valuable SEAL experience was still around the corner, and I was anxious to get home to my son who had been born while I was on deployment. He was four months old before I laid eyes on his beautiful face.

When I returned from Afghanistan in 2002, I got into training—into advanced sniper training specifically. Usually you have a choice or some say in your next assignment, but I was overseas and this decision was made for me. The SEAL community was growing, and they consolidated training under one command called Training Detachment. During my brief tour I was in charged of urban and helicopter sniper training for all the West Coast SEAL snipers. It was rewarding work, and I often got to invent and write curriculum and then teach it. Guys like Chris Kyle would come through our advanced courses (rural, waterborne, and other training was taught as well).

Then the phone rang one day. I had no idea how that single thread in time would forever alter my career and life.

Senior Chief Nelson called up to the advanced training command: "Hey, we're modernizing our basic sniper program, and I need a couple of experienced guys to represent the West Coast and augment a pilot course." Those "two guys" ended up being Eric Davis and me. In the SEAL teams we have our own sniper course; it's three months long, and is now one of the best in the world. Before two former SEAL Team 6 men decided to make it so (Manty and Nelson), it was antiquated and had a very negative teaching style. This would change, and for the better.

Senior Chief Nelson continued, "We want you to come down and be part of the cadre to really bring the SEAL sniper course into the 21st century."

I went down and augmented the sniper pilot course, and had a blast working with the other SEALs from the East Coast. Shortly after, Senior Chief Nelson convinced me to give up my orders as a SEAL BUD/S instructor to help out his staff. "I need good guys," he said.

Now let me tell you something: Being a BUD/S instructor is one of the best jobs in the world. You work out, teach a bit, and have a pretty normal 9-5 schedule. OK, maybe it's more 5-5, but it's an incredible job.

You take on an army of potential SEAL students, of which 90 percent will quit. It's an incredibly negative environment, on purpose, and is designed to see who has the internal tools and fortitude to push themselves through training at all costs. Those who will never give up, no matter what is thrown at them.

In my class, we started with over 220, and graduated 23 originals.

For us SEALs, this job is kind of like taking a break. You work about three days a week, yell at some students, have them wash your car on the weekends, and finish your undergrad or graduate degree. It's also a chance to kind of decompress.

So I gave that all up, for me and my family, in order to go down and work with Senior Chief Nelson. It was the most demanding and rewarding assignment of my naval career. My biggest reward was learning the true value of how powerful our internal thought process really is. It all started with a trip to meet with a mental-management guru.

We were scheduled to meet a guy named Lanny Basham for a few days in Arizona at one of those really bad hotels with the cramped conference rooms and bad lighting. We all know the type: the same picture of the deer on the wall, at every hotel, in every state. Not exactly a great environment in which to learn.

SEALs are skeptics by nature, but also early adopters if they see it's truly a great idea or product. When I heard we were being flown to Arizona to hear a talk on mental management, I rolled my eyes with the rest of the guys attending. All that would change the minute Lanny started to tell his story.

He wasn't a very athletic kid, but he had a great father who told him something significant we can all learn from: "Everyone has gifts: Your job is to figure out what your gifts are, Lanny." I wish every parent was this wise!

Lanny's gift was competitive shooting. He would ultimately go on to win a world championship, then be the first loser, a close second, or silver, at his event in the Olympics.

He was devastated. Everyone (including himself) expected him to win the gold medal. He eventually realized what had held him back was what he was thinking and saying to himself internally. He got rattled by a few Russian guys in the competition who were giving him a hard time on the bus ride out to the event. That's when he started talking to himself, and not in a good way.

How many of us can relate to that? Sports, public speaking, class projects, job interviews? What we think, and how we talk to ourselves, matters. Always.

Lanny nudged me into thinking about how to teach differently. When I eventually got put in charge of the sniper program as course manager, I adopted a positive style of teaching for our students versus a negative style. Let me explain.

Negative style: "Hey Adam! You suck! What are you doing?! You're flinching every time you pull the trigger on that rifle!"

Positive style: "Hey Adam, relax a bit. Remember your fundamentals, nice and smooth on your trigger pull. OK?"

Two very different approaches. Which one do you think is the most powerful? What approach do you think produces powerful, positive internal "self" conversations?

So how did we take a 70 percent graduation rate to a 95 percent graduation rate? Let me reiterate, these were Navy SEAL sniper students, accomplished SEALs, that would come to the course, and still we were losing 30 percent of them!

Unacceptable, I thought. Here are the three things we did, and also three very powerful lessons in thinking that you can apply to your own life, and how you talk to other people—especially kids.

One: We implemented a positive over negative teaching style.

If you're coaching somebody or teaching somebody something for the first time, it does no good to point out all the mistakes this person is making when you can instead focus on telling them what to do right. After all, beginners are still learning. Why program them with mistakes?

You see a lot of negative teaching out there, like in military boot camp. There, that has a purpose, but such a negative approach does not apply to most things in life. Following Lanny's instruction, we began changing the way we talked to the students, interacting with them in a more positive, productive way. Lanny had illustrated an important point: How we think about ourselves can have a dramatic effect on our performance and tenacity.

And just to back up a bit, when we were in the process of modernizing the sniper course, we went and surveyed the best sniper programs in the U.S., and then we went to the Olympic arena and focused on gold-medalist champions (thank you, Lanny). We wanted to know what the gold medalists were doing. We didn't want to focus on silver or bronze, the second or third; we wanted to know what makes up the champions and what they were doing differently. We looked at professional sports, and that's where we gleaned many of the principles we later implemented in our course. I learned later that thinking powerfully can create change in all aspects of our lives.

The positive over negative aspect was extremely important. I use this today in my own business, when I talk to my team or when I'm training somebody. I watch how I talk to them, as well as how I speak to my own children. It's so important.

Two: We encouraged mental visualization or mental rehearsal.

How many of us really take the time to close our eyes and visualize ourselves practicing or performing? Who's practiced this before? If you have, then good for you—you're halfway there.

We taught our students how to practice perfectly in their heads. This brings us back to another Lanny story, this one about a guy he called Captain Jack Sands.

Jack was a Navy fighter pilot who was shot down right at the beginning of the Vietnam conflict, and spent over six years in Hanoi Hilton—a POW camp for those of you who don't know. Jack came back six-plus years later, was flown into San Diego, and was then put in the ambulance to go to Balboa Hospital to get checked out because he was in terrible shape. He was so malnourished, he probably weighed barely 100 pounds while standing over six feet tall.

They drove him past the golf course, out of the back gate of the naval air station, where he made the ambulance driver stop. He said, "Wait, stop. Stop the ambulance."

"What are you talking about?"

Jack said, "I've got to play golf! I've been golfing in my head for six years. I've got to play golf!"

So that was what Jack did. When he was a POW, he would play all his favorite golf courses in his mind. He was playing these rounds of golf for six years, perfectly.

He got out of the ambulance and approached the clubhouse. Right away, they tried to throw him out because he looked like hell.

"What are you doing here, buddy?" they asked.

He told them his story. These guys embraced him with tears in their eyes, took him to the pro shop, and outfitted him to the hilt.

He said, "I want to shoot 18 holes." So out he went and he shot his first round of golf in over six years, 18 holes, and he shoots a par.

Naturally, these guys were looking at him like *how is this possible*? He said, "Fellas, I don't know what to tell you. I've been playing perfect golf in my head for six years."

If that isn't an example of powerful thinking, I don't know what is.

This story really reinforces why thinking, focusing, and talking to ourselves positively is so important; you can literally practice whatever you can think of in your head, and practice it to perfection.

I remember the first time I told our instructors to start telling our students that we expected them to shoot perfect scores. We had an instructor/mentor program. Our students would always ask us, "What are you expecting out of us on this first shooting test?" We started saying, "We want you to shoot 100 percent because you can." And they did.

When I started talking to my students like that, they started shooting perfectly. Even the other instructors were impressed. It became a competition among the staff: We were each assigned four students, and you didn't want to show up Monday morning and look over the roster to find your guys at the bottom of the student list. Incentives are everything.

I remember giving my students—Adam and Ted, both funny guys and extremely talented—all these CDs on mental management to listen to. (This was back when CDs were a thing. Today, my 12-year-old has no idea what a CD is!) These two SEALs would go into their rental car every night and listen to those CDs. The rest of the students would give them such a hard time.

"What are you guys doing? Making out in the car together?"

Little did they know, Ted and Adam would have the last laugh.

These guys could shoot. Just to give you an idea of how hard the standards are, the first weapon system that we test these guys on is a .308 semi-automatic rifle, and we test them at ranges of up to 1,000 meters, which is right at the envelope of the weapon's performance limitations.

They go through two tests, each of them as a shooter and a spotter. We grade the shooter and the spotter in both cases. We have a snaps and movers test where they go from 200, 400, 600, and 800 meters, and they're hitting multiple targets moving left and right, head shots in rapid succession.

Then they go to an unknown-distance range where they have to very quickly assess the distance and range it with their scopes—no technology allowed—and then they have to shoot that. In addition to that challenge, you have these incredible variables to contend with such as wind and atmospheric conditions.

So there are all these variables, and these two guys shooting their first rifle test scored 100 percent, 100 percent, 95 percent, and 100 percent. At the end of the day, there was a line outside their barracks room to get those CDs.

This is where I saw, right in front of me, the power of thought, and it became extremely important to me in everything I do.

Three: We taught the guys how to self-coach.

We encouraged them to take time to think through obstacles and to talk themselves through overcoming it. This is so important,

because we all walk around and think to ourselves and talk to ourselves in a certain way:

"I'm not good at math."

"I'm not a very good golfer."

"I'm not very flexible."

"I'm a terrible dancer."

"I'm not good with kids."

I could go on, but you get the idea. These are all self-created
limiting factors, and if you think of yourself in this way, you'll in-
evitably become it. How we think about things and how we think
about ourselves really matters. If you think something is possible
or not possible, you're right in both cases.

I experienced the crippling effects of self-doubt when I went to
advanced SEAL training. Keep in mind, I grew up on a sailboat in
California; I'd never shot a gun before in my life.

So here I am, having just graduated SEAL training with class
215, about to go on to advanced SEAL training—a three-month
tactical course where you really learn how to be a SEAL and apply
all the cool-guy skills. It was here that I hit a major road block.

I was a terrible shot.

I was really struggling. In fact, it was no secret that I was the
worst shot in the class. And I was having these terrible thoughts in
my head like, "Oh my God, how am I going to overcome this? How
could I be this bad?!" Then I remember having a breakthrough. I
started thinking more powerfully. I said to myself, "Just reset. You
have the ability to be a good shot, just become a good shot. In fact,
you can be the best shot in the class."

I started changing the way I thought about myself and then,
with practice and patience, I progressed and became one of the best
shots in the class.

Then I became one of the best shots in GOLF platoon, my first
SEAL platoon at SEAL Team 3.

Then I was selected for sniper school.

We've all had friends who talk to themselves and say, "I'm
just an average golfer," "I'm not a good swimmer," "I'm not a good
this, not a good that...." If you're having that conversation with

yourself, you're really setting a glass ceiling and preventing your-self from ever becoming exceptional.

So we started talking to the students about how they coach themselves. You really have to change the way they think about things and how they talk to themselves and have those conversa-tions. All of that stuff took a 70 percent graduation rate up to 99 percent, and it just stayed there. When we implemented the pow-erful thinking into the sniper course, we started graduating nearly everybody. We'd lose a guy here and there, but the results spoke for themselves.

Consider what I'm about to tell you as a cautionary tale, like the old warnings of years past found deep in some South American jungle (take your pick), carved into stone in some old ruins and translated as, "All who enter, do so and risk your own peril." Yes, you've been warned. Hopefully you take something valuable away from my experiences facing adversity with powerful thinking and turning it into leverage for success, happiness, and more.

When I left the military, it was to become my own boss. It didn't work out so well at first, but after a few false starts, including getting kicked in the teeth a couple of times, I finally found something that I enjoyed doing—writing and publishing—and I turned it into a business. But it didn't start out so well! And like most things in life, there are incredible lessons in failure that, like college credits, are requirements to become successful by our own measure.

I was a 29-year-old Navy SEAL chief petty officer with a young family. I made over a quarter million dollars buying small houses and apartments while on active duty, and I was hooked on real estate (always a great investment if you buy right). That led me to start reading books on investing and business (a good place to start for anyone). If you want to be successful, start reading about other successful people and their experiences. Then I did some simple military retirement math, and realized that if I stuck around another 7-12 years (this would put me at 20 or 25 years in), I wouldn't just be physically broken, I'd be financially broke as well. I had great income as a Navy SEAL because of all the special pays that added to my base pay, but only my base pay would factor into my retirement pay, so in essence, I would get the same retirement as a Navy cook (no offense, Navy cooks!). Hopefully this changes in the future, but it was that way in 2006 when I took the jump and left active duty for the civilian world.

So there I was, on active duty; I'd been meritoriously promoted to E6 at our training detachment sniper cell, then recruited to the SEAL sniper course by an old SEAL Team 6 senior chief, and then selected for chief petty officer my first at-bat while acting as the West Coast sniper course manager. I had a great career, but my fun meter was pegged, my back was killing me, and I wanted a better life for my family. I jumped from a speeding train.

It was one of the best decisions I ever made.

I spent some time contracting overseas with a three-letter U.S. agency to put some money away, then started writing a business plan (my first ever, but needed for any venture, trust me) with a SEAL buddy of mine, Randy, who later became my business partner. What was the business? We saw the massive need for training areas for military, law enforcement and first responders in California. We were going to raise a few million dollars, buy a thousand acres, and develop it into a driving track and some shooting ranges. In hindsight it was a crazy first business venture, but SEALs don't know the word no.

To make a long story longer, we did buy that land, raised just under $4M, and got the property through a complex and expensive county planning process in just under four years. However, saying it was a tumultuous process would be an understatement.

I have to pause for a laugh out loud here. I once had an ambitious and misguided young local reporter call me to inquire about some of my "Tumultuous business dealings...." I've got news for you, if you're in business, especially as an owner, stand by for rapids around the corner! It's part of being in business. Anyone who says otherwise is a politician or a reporter with no business experience.

Randy and I parted ways (we're still good friends) following an influx of new partners, and after the project was finally approved, the San Diego, California chapter of the Sierra Club sued the county over our project's environmental impact report. It's a common tactic to kill projects or drag them out. Unfortunately for us, it choked the life out of the project.

It was a complete failure, and as the CEO and co-founder, I had to accept full responsibility for it. (I've learned that it's much easier to just accept responsibility and admit fault rather than put it off. Avoiding it just makes it much worse.)

So I walked away from it all. I had my entire net worth tied up in the project, as well as money from friends and family, and soon after, my wife asked me for a divorce. I feel like divorce is the elephant in the room nobody wants to acknowledge. Over half the population in North America is divorced, and the legal system sets the stage for a knock-down, bar room-style brawl that leaves both sides angry, bitter, and broke. If there are kids involved, it's worse, but it doesn't have to be.

My wife (at the time), and I were in counseling when she had the courage to end the marriage (I was in denial), and we decided, with help from our psychiatrist, to have a happy divorce. This was an easy enough decision, but extremely hard to execute. Still, we did it.

I remember when she told me she wanted to move the kids three counties away to her family's ranch in northern California. I freaked out and got really mad. Then, I was reminded that her happiness and feeling safe would help our children deal with the situation. Happy mom equals happy kids. Such an important point.

So I ignored my legal rights and did what was right for my children and my ex-wife's happiness. Fighting and trash-talking each other just makes it worse for everyone. If there are children involved, you and your partner are co-parents for life, and you have a decision to make.

I remember when things were really tough and emotions were running high, our counselor gave us two scenarios to think about. One involved a vicious divorce where nobody won, and the kids suffered. The other version was a vision of two people who cared about their children, put their differences aside to support each other's happiness, and created a loving environment and positive example for their children (and their families). It worked.

By taking time to think about the consequences and long-term effects of our actions, and how this would determine outcomes, we made a decision to support each other. So, we sat down and made a list of what each of us wanted: kids' schedule, money, assets, house, the list goes on. It wasn't easy, but we worked it all out with our psychiatrist and then, and only then, we went to a lawyer to have our agreement drafted up and executed. Note: I've been to several counselors, and nothing beats a PhD. There's just no substitute for it. Period. You may think you'll save money by visiting a less-qualified counselor, but in the long run, it's much cheaper to suck it up and pay the money for a real psychiatrist. If you think it's expensive, just remind yourself how much money you're saving in attorney fees by going this route.

Now I realize some of you may be shaking your heads in disbelief because this is not a common practice in divorce; most people lawyer-up and let the fireworks begin. Think about it for a second: Who knows what's best for you and your children? Two attorneys interpreting state law, incentivized to fight and rack up legal fees? Or the two of you?

And we were honest with our kids about what was happening.

I still remember taking our kids to a park (we picked somewhere we'd likely never go to again) and how their mom and I sat them down and gave them the honest, cold, hard truth. Some of the hardest words I've ever uttered were, "Your mom and I love you very much, but we've decided it's best to not be together as husband and wife. We still love and care about each other and you, and we are all still a family." I could barely get the words out without breaking down in tears. To be completely honest, I cried like a baby, long and hard by myself, afterward. Nothing wrong with this at all. Real men cry, Navy SEALs included.

It's not a common thing we did, and we ended up having an uncommon, but positive, outcome because of it—one that resulted in the two of us being close friends, having good relationships with each other's families, and being great co-parents together. I just had Thanksgiving with her, her husband, and all of our children at my friend's farm in Portland, Oregon, and it was amazing. I also have a great relationship with her family, as she does with mine. We all support each other and the kids have benefited from it. Our children are happy, independent, doing incredible in school, and excelling at their chosen interests. People comment to me about my relationship with my ex and kids all the time, so I thought it important to share this experience with you because so many divorces end in ruin. If there are children involved, they ultimately suffer.

Again, taking the time to think about the consequences of my decisions and visualizing them play out, good and bad, made a huge difference in our decision to do this. The power of thought at work again.

That said, if there was ever a lower point in my life than when I lost all my money and my wife, I don't remember it. Up until this point, I had turned many "you'll never do that, it's too difficult" naysayers into believers.

Now, I was a living country music song.

Shortly after this I filed for unemployment, and felt even worse! Navy SEAL to unemployment line. It was extremely embarrassing for me, and brought me straight back to elementary school and having to stand up with the few other welfare kids, in front of the entire class each day, to collect our free lunch tickets. That was one of the most embarrassing rituals I can remember as a kid.

So here I was, the worst low I can remember, but it proved to be among the most pivotal moments of my life. I remembered, by thinking back to what worked on our sniper students, the power of thought. I just had to take the time to think—yes, just think—about what really mattered to me. It all became OK again very quickly. As my friend Kamal Ravikant writes in his book *Love Yourself Like Your Life Depends On It*, I just had to start loving myself again.

My children loved me, their mom and I were getting along, everyone was healthy in my family, and that's what was most important at the moment.

I started thinking about all the positives in my life: good friends, family, and skills I acquired inside and outside of the SEAL teams that I could rely on to start over. When I started thinking in a positive way again, things started to look different and get a whole lot better.

I love the Japanese proverb, "Fall down six times, get up seven." It's one of the most important lessons I learned in business and the SEAL teams. Like I said earlier, failure is an important part of success. In fact, the ladder of success and happiness is built with the rungs of failure.

I had a choice: I could feel sorry for myself (maybe jump off the Coronado Bridge) or I could reflect on all the valuable mistakes I'd made, and use the experience to better myself in my relationships and in my next business venture.

After all, I'd had some success; my partners and I raised $3.8M dollars in a down economy, I understood the difference between debt and equity financing, how an LLC had more flexibility than a C corporation, and the importance of choosing good partners. I had failed miserably, but I had also received an MBA in the process and had experience that couldn't be taught in the classroom or learned on a spreadsheet.

My luck was about to change, and it was due to powerful thinking, hard work, and perseverance. Within a few months, I had landed on my feet with an offer from a large defense company, and I was making more money than I could have ever imagined. They needed a special ops guy with an active security clearance to help manage a classified contract with the government, and interface between the client and engineers. Those smart engineers are always spending R&D money on their own good ideas, but usually the customer wants their ideas built! This was where I learned to always listen to what the customer wants, because chances are it's different from what you want.

So that was my job: Keep the customer happy; make upgrades they want, not what the engineers want; and land new business. It was a great job and experience. My boss was a tough and intelligent female; I had nothing but respect for her. But within a year I knew the corporate world wasn't for me. I was itching for entrepreneurship.

Working in the defense industry from the other side was very interesting. There's so much abuse and fixed monopoly involved in government contracting. The Federal Acquisition Regulations (FAR) are a good guideline, but it's very complex and rife for rigging. Thankfully the company I was with actually cared about their work, and they played fair. But playing fair sometimes means you lose business, especially in the world of defense contracting.

Back when my first start-up was getting really stressful, I started to write. I wrote fiction for a few magazines, and actually got paid for it. Then I starting writing rifle reviews as well. Writing and storytelling was something I really started to enjoy as a creative outlet and stress reliever.

Around this time, a former student of mine from the sniper course, Marcus Luttrell, had just come out with a book called "Lone Survivor." I remembered talking to Marcus—we talked about a lot of things, including writing—and he was actually one of the first guys who suggested I write my own story. I was hesitant because that decision would surely come with inside baseball SEAL drama; I'd seen the heat Marcus had taken from our own community. We're the worst at times, and are often the first to eat our own.

Then something changed. I watched a video on YouTube called "The Last Lecture." It was about a university professor with a young family who suddenly developed terminal cancer. In his last talk, which he filmed, he explained his life's journey up to that point and all the lessons he'd learned, all for his kids to later watch. It was very moving. I cried like a baby because it hit home; I'd lost so many friends in the SEAL teams, and experienced so many close calls. I wanted to leave something for my own kids so that my oldest son, who was born after 9/11 when I was in Afghanistan, and his sister and brother would know how tough it all was on Mom and Dad. That, and I knew I had many lessons to pass on.

So right before I lost everything I cared about in life, I decided I was going to write a book. After a brief run-in with a writer/scam artist who promised me the world, I finally struck out on my own. I read some books on how to get published, and then started calling agents. I was turned down by dozens before I found one. Then my agent and I were turned down by at least five or six publishers before Marc Resnic at St. Martin's Press took a gamble on me.

They gave me a $25,000 advance to finish the manuscript, and at my agent's advice ("It's a memoir, get help," she said, and she was right), I brought on a writing partner, John Mann. John and I continue to write together to this day. He's an amazing writer, incredible, and I owe much of my own improvement in my writing style to his own mastery of the written word. Want to get better at something? Hang out with the best!

The Red Circle came out in early 2012 alongside my friend Chris Kyle's book *American Sniper*, and it made the New York

Times best-seller list in the first week. It has since sold over one hundred thousand copies. It's published in a few foreign languages, too.

At the time I was selling my story, no one gave a crap about SEALs or their books. The biggest, and only, SEAL hit was *Rogue Warrior* by Richard "Dick" Marcinko, founder of SEAL Team 6. Up to that point, SEALs and other spec ops guys just hadn't seen much action or had that much to write about. September 11th changed all that. All of a sudden, special operations, once the ugly step-brother of the U.S. military, was now the crown prince of the Department of Defense. The Navy SEALs, through some luck (remember what I said before about powerful thinking, hard work, and perseverance influencing luck), would find themselves on some of the most successful operations in the history of modern warfare, with killing Osama bin Laden at the top of the list.

My book did well, and I was pleased, but another momentous change came around that time that has influenced my life perhaps more greatly.

Shortly before my book came out, I was still working in the defense industry, and had started blogging part time for a big military website. I'd become very good at it. I really enjoyed short-form writing, the instant gratification of seeing a post do well, and the ability to engage with an online audience. It was here that I met a friend and fellow writer named Jack Murphy, a combat veteran of the Army's Rangers and Special Forces. Jack is a great writer who has self-published quite a few novels and co-wrote with me the New York Times best-seller *Benghazi: The Definitive Report*.

I noticed something while blogging at this big site that made a lot of money associating themselves with the military. They really didn't care that much about the military community. I slowly became disenfranchised, and eventually left to start my own website. I asked Jack to join me. He thought I was crazy at first, but agreed to go along for the ride. We both had no idea how big SOFREP. com (Special Operations Forces Report) would become, or that it would provide us both with meaningful employment.

The defense company I was working for gave me a leave of absence during *The Red Circle* book tour in 2012, which proved to be the perfect time to launch my SOFREP experiment. I'd noticed while blogging for the other military website that there was an intense interest in the world of special operations. Video games like *Call of Duty* were crushing it, movies like *Act of Valor* and *Lone Survivor* were smash hits, and yet there was no legitimate Internet site in 2012 that addressed the world of special operations.

I spent weekends locked inside my apartment for a month straight, working through the night, turning my napkin sketch of SOFREP into reality—naming it, designing the logo, writing content, recruiting others to write. In February of 2012 we launched. We had over a million views our first month.

Skip forward, and today SOFREP is under the umbrella of Force12 Media, a digital media company specializing in news and men's lifestyle content, all anchored firmly in the world of military and special operations.

The name Force12 comes from the sea; it's related to a nautical storm rating scale, 12 being a typhoon- or hurricane-strength storm. "Media by storm" is our tag line. Our websites, podcasts, online clubs, and book-publishing imprint (with MacMillan publishing) reaches tens of millions of people monthly. In 2014, I turned down an offer of $15 million to purchase it all; it wasn't a good fit for us culturally.

So how did I go from training snipers to running a digital media business? Crazy right? It all started with a thought.

Today I live in the American commonwealth of San Juan, Puerto Rico, and travel to and from a small home office in Manhattan where I spend some time tethered to the center of the media world. I live a great life. New York is one of the best cities in the world, and my home in San Juan is on a beautiful island. Puerto Ricans are some of the friendliest I've encountered in all my travels. My kids love it down there.

Owning my own business and schedule also allows me to see my kids often, and take them on crazy adventures. I talk to them regularly about our most valuable asset—time—and the power of thinking for themselves in life.

Even at a young age my children understand the power of thought. I see it in everything they do in their lives. It's an amazing thing to see them excel in academics and sports, using the philosophy of champions to better themselves.

———— ◆ ————

A few years ago, I started getting invited to speak at events held by companies like Nike, Lone Star Eye Clinic, Stansberry Research, and others. After sharing my life's experiences, especially about my time in the SEAL sniper course, people kept coming up to me begging me to write a book about it all. So like any good SEAL would, I decided to exceed expectations and write two books! The one you're reading now, and a much bigger one published by Penguin that comes out sometime in 2016/17. The latter book will reveal more of my experiences and in greater detail.

So why write this book now and not wait? Sometimes we writers just have something inside of us we need to get out. This was one of those times. I couldn't stop thinking (fitting, given the title of this book) about it; the concept was keeping me up at night and interfering with the first novel I was writing. So, to cure my sleep problem, I decided to just finally write *The Power of Thought* and get it out of me.

I wrote this book in my San Juan condominium, nonstop through two nights straight. I put the final touches to it while riding on airplanes back and forth from Puerto Rico to New York.

I can finally sleep again.

I wrote this book because I realized that the concept of thinking powerfully can and should be shared beyond the U.S. Navy SEAL teams, pro sports, and Olympic champions. Because all of us have the gift of thought inside of us, we just have to use it, believe in it, and start thinking more powerfully in our lives.

With it, we can overcome any challenge.

The power of thought is real.

OTHER BOOKS BY BRANDON WEBB

Navy SEAL Sniper

The Red Circle

Among Heroes

Benghazi: The Definitive Report

The Killing School

ABOUT THE AUTHOR

Brandon Webb is a former U.S. Navy SEAL, author, digital-media entrepreneur and CEO of Force12 Media.

After leaving home at age 16, Brandon finished high school and joined the U.S. Navy to become a Navy SEAL. His first permanent assignment was as a helicopter aircrew search and rescue (SAR) swimmer and aviation warfare systems operator with HS-6. In 1997, his Basic Underwater Demolition/SEAL (BUD/S) package was approved. He would class up with over 200 students in BUD/S class 215, and go on to complete the training as one of 23 originals.

As a SEAL, he served with SEAL TEAM 3, Naval Special Warfare Group One (NSWG-1) Training Detachment sniper cell, and completed his last tour at the Naval Special Warfare Center (NSWC) sniper course, where he served as the West Coast sniper course manager. During his career he completed four deployments to the Middle East and would later go back to Iraq in 2006-7 as a paramilitary contractor. His proudest accomplishment in the military was working as the SEAL sniper course manager, a schoolhouse that has produced some of the deadliest snipers in U.S. military history.

An accomplished leader, Brandon was meritoriously promoted to E-6 while serving as an advanced sniper instructor at NSWG-1, and was recommended and promoted to the rank of chief petty officer (E-7) his first time eligible during his tenure at the NSWC sniper course. He has received numerous distinguished service awards including the Presidential Unit Citation (personally awarded to him by President George W. Bush), and the Navy and Marine Corps Commendation medal with "V" device for valor in combat. Webb ended his Navy career after over a decade of service in order to spend more time with his children.

After the Navy he served briefly as a contractor supporting U.S. intelligence interests in northern Iraq, and then transitioned to full-time writing and entrepreneurship around 2008.

Today, Brandon is focused on pursuing his career in media, and as a writer. He is the founder of Force12 Media, a digital publishing company that reaches tens of millions monthly, and is the largest military content network on the Internet.

Brandon is a New York Times best-selling author, and is regularly featured in international media as a military and special operations subject matter expert. He has contributed to ABC's Good Morning America, NBC's Today Show, FOX news, CNN, the BBC, SIRIUS XM, MSNBC, and The New York Times.

In 2012, after losing his best friend, Navy SEAL and CIA contractor Glen Doherty, in Benghazi, Libya, he founded The Red Circle Foundation (RCF), a non-profit with a 100 percent pass-through model; every dollar donated goes to the mission, and business partners pick up the foundation's overhead. RCF is focused on supporting families of the special operations community through emergency memorial, medical, and child-enrichment programs (camps and scholarships).

Brandon enjoys spending time with his amazing children, being outdoors, and flying his planes upside-down. He splits his time between his home in San Juan, Puerto Rico, and his Manhattan, New York, home office.

Twitter & Instagram: @BrandonTwebb

Blog: BrandonTylerWebb.com

I'd consider it an honor to have you review this book for me on Amazon and elsewhere.

Sincerely,
Brandon

Made in the USA
Monee, IL
20 March 2020